billie jean king THE LADY OF THE COURT

By James T. Olsen
Illustrated By John Nelson

Text copyright © 1974 by Educreative Systems, Inc. Illustrations copyright © 1974 by Creative Education. International copyrights reserved in all countries. No part of this book may be reproduced in any form without written permission from the publisher. Printed in the United States. Library of Congress Number: 73-12438   ISBN: 0-87191-275-9

Published by Creative Education, Mankato, Minnesota 56001
Prepared for the Publisher by Educreative Systems, Inc.
Distributed by Childrens Press, 1224 West Van Buren Street, Chicago, Illinois 60607

Library of Congress Cataloging in Publication Data
James T. Olsen
Billie Jean King; the lady of the court.
(The Superstars)
SUMMARY: A biography of a champion, winner of almost every amateur tennis title in the world, whose present interests include bringing tennis to ghetto children and Women's Lib to the tennis court.
1. King, Billie Jean—Juvenile literature. [1. King, Billie Jean. 2. Tennis—Biography]
I. Nelson, John, illus. II. Title.
GV994.K56E38 796.34'2'0924 [B] [92] 73-12438 ISBN 0-87191-275-9

A white ball flies across a net. People cheer. They are cheering an 18 year old girl who looks hot. The sun shines on her glasses and her short, wavy brown hair. As the 5 foot 6 inch girl races towards the sidelines, the people see a lot of freckles on a shiny, happy face. Smack! The ball flies again.

"Little Miss Moffitt" has just won the first round of the All-England Championship at Wimbledon.

The year was 1962 and "Little Miss Moffitt" was a little known girl who would later be known as Billie Jean King, the best woman tennis player in the world. She surprised everyone by beating Margaret Smith of Australia. Billie Jean was to go from that victory to many more. She has since held almost every amateur tennis title in the world.

Billie Jean was born on November 22, 1943, in Long Beach, California. Her father, William J. Moffitt, worked as an engineer for the fire department and her mother worked as a receptionist.

From the time Billie Jean was a small child, she had done very well at all sports. Billie Jean was a shortstop for a girl's softball team. Her father says that at the Fire Department picnics the men wanted her to play shortstop or third base. They would fight over which team she was to play on. Everyone could see, even then, that she was terrific. She could handle a bat, field, and throw. As a matter of fact, Billie Jean was a natural for a job as a professional ball player.

But there was a problem. As she grew up, she began to understand that she would have little or no chance of making it in baseball. She realized that women were not accepted as baseball players. If she wanted to be a great athlete, baseball was not the sport for her. She wanted to find a sport "where you could still be considered a lady." Her parents tried to help Billie Jean. They all talked about her problem a lot. Finally, the Moffitts agreed that Billie Jean was right; there was little chance for her in baseball. Then they told her that she might be able to have a future in tennis. That was a game that both girls and boys could play.

Billie decided to give tennis a chance. When she was eleven years old, her father enrolled her in

a tennis program given by the city of Long Beach. Her parents were not too sure that Billie would be happy with tennis, though. They were afraid that she would get tired of the game. They didn't think she would find tennis as exciting a sport as baseball was. Neither of her parents had ever played tennis. They weren't tennis fans either. They had no idea how fast, hard, and challenging a game of tennis was. The Moffitts shouldn't have worried about Billie Jean. She seemed to love tennis. During the summer when she was on vacation from school, she played tennis all day long. She couldn't seem to get enough of it. There was always something new to learn. While she was in high school, it was the same way. She would play tennis all the time, every single chance she got. She began to talk about being a tennis champion, and this idea became her main goal in life. She said she was going to become good enough to play at Wimbledon.

Her parents were very surprised. Billie Jean never seemed to get tired of playing tennis. Billie Jean bought her first tennis racket with money she earned by doing odd jobs in her neighborhood. It took her months to save up the money, but she didn't seem to mind. At this time, she also decided that if she was going to be a good tennis player, she would have to build up her body. So she walked three and a half miles to school every day to build up her leg muscles. She knew that she must have strong legs to move fast enough, often enough, to keep hitting the ball over the net. Every day she spent hours and hours hitting balls over the net. She practiced hard to improve her serve and to improve her stroke. She knew she needed speed and accuracy. The ball not only had to be sent back over the net, but Billie Jean had to make the ball land exactly where she wanted it to. She gave so much time to tennis that she didn't have time to give to the simple fun of growing up. Tennis was her fun. Tennis was her life. Being a champion tennis player was her goal.

One time, in an interview, Billie Jean was asked what gave her the strength and energy to play such a hard game. She told a story about her grandparents. There were some from Scotland, Ireland and England. And one who was an American Seminole Indian. Billie Jean said that it was her Indian blood that gave her

the stamina to play the tough, tiring game of tennis that had made her famous.

At this time in her life, Billie Jean had a hero. He was not a tennis player. And he was not a baseball player, either. He was the Reverend Bob Richards, the Minister of the First Church of the Brethren. This was the church Billie Jean and her family went to. Besides being a minister, Reverend Richards was also an Olympics-winning pole vaulter. He talked with Billie Jean and encouraged her to practice her tennis playing. He was a really fine athlete and that was what Billie Jean wanted to be. So Billie Jean used him as a model.

Billie Jean learned her lessons well. At the ripe old age of eleven she played her first major tennis match

against Marilyn Hester, who was in her second year at the University of Southern California. Billie Jean won the match 6-3, 6-4. When Billie Jean was fifteen years old the great tennis star, Alice Marble, offered to give Billie Jean tennis lessons. Billie Jean was pleased and excited that a great tennis star like Miss Marble wanted to give her lessons. She stayed with Alice Marble for about six months. They worked together every weekend. The lessons were very helpful because Billie Jean learned as much as she could from Miss Marble. Miss Marble had a lot of faith in Billie Jean. She was a great tennis star, and she thought Billie Jean could be great, too. She wanted Billie to learn a great deal from her. Billie Jean didn't let Miss Marble down. After the lessons were finished, Billie's national ranking as a tennis player went from nineteenth to fourth. Billie was on her way.

Billie Jean won her first title in 1958. Then she won the Southern California Championship in her age group. She then went on to play in the National Girl's 15 and Under Championship in Middletown, Ohio. But she was unlucky then, and she lost in the quarter finals. Of course, she was terribly disappointed. The reason for her disappointment is interesting. She herself says: "When I started playing in tournaments, my game had its ups and downs. But I learned an all-around game, and it paid off, even though I suffered. Now a lot of children don't realize this, or they realize but can't stand to lose. It used to just kill me! But I felt in the long run that if I really wanted to make my goals I would have to lose."

Billie Jean hated to lose. But she felt that you have to lose to know how to win. She knew that it takes time to learn a sport well. And Billie knew that while she was learning there would be times when she would lose. But if she learned her mistakes and learned to correct them she had a better chance to win. When Billie Jean played for a championship, she felt she had learned enough to get that far and that she would win. To lose then, "just killed her."

The following year she played against Brazil's Maria Bueno, the holder of the 1959 Wimbledon title. The match was played in South Orange, New Jersey and Billie Jean lost it. She was very upset because she

wanted to see if she could, in fact, beat a Wimbledon champ. In the crowd of people who had seen the match, there was a man by the name of Frank Brennan. Frank Brennan had watched the match carefully. And even though Billie Jean had lost, he thought she had played very well. He believed that she could play much better than she had, too. He knew that she needed more training, teaching, practicing, and coaching. He thought that she was a player who could be a real champ some day. He also wondered why Billie Jean had played with a tennis racket that was strung with nylon instead of gut. He asked Billie. Billie said that she didn't have the money to buy gut string for her racket. So she had to make do with what she could buy.

Brennan decided to become Billie's coach. He wanted to work with Billie, teach her. Help her to become the champion she wanted to be. Brennan ran a tennis center in Saddle River, New Jersey and he thought that Billie should study tennis with him there. She did. And the lessons were good.

They were so good that in 1960 Billie reached the finals of the National Girls' 18 and Under Championships. But Billie was not to win this time either. She lost to Karen Hantze. In the following year she and Miss Hantze teamed up and became the youngest pair ever to win the women's doubles title at Wimbledon.

Shortly after this match, Billie Jean decided that she would go to college. She chose to go to Los Angeles State College. The problem with college was that her studies left her very little time to practice tennis. Billie Jean wouldn't give up, though. She worked extra hard and made the time to study and play tennis.

In 1962, she beat Margaret Smith at the Wimbledon matches in England. She was invited to England again in 1963. This time she made the single's finals at Wimbledon. On the way to this victory Billie Jean beat three other players, who had been playing for much longer than she had. But in the final match she lost to Margaret Smith. After the game was over, Miss Smith told Billie, "You know, Billie Jean, you've got all the shots but I always wear you out. I know you don't practice. I KNOW YOU COULD win Wimbledon. Why don't you give it a go?" Billie knew that Miss Smith was right. Her studies had taken time away from her tennis. But Billie wanted to finish college.

There was an important personal reason Billie wanted to stay in college. At college she had met Larry King. She had fallen in love with him and she wanted to spend time with Larry as well as play tennis and study. In the fall of 1964, she and Larry were engaged to be married. After the engagement, Billie left for Australia to spend three months training with Mervyn Rose.

Mervyn Rose was a very good teacher. He knew Billie Jean and he knew just the kind of lessons that she needed. First, he put her through daily exercises and drills to build up her strength. What Miss Smith had said about Billie "wearing out" was true, and Rose was the man who ended that problem. Secondly, Rose made Billie Jean shorten all of her strokes. He shortened her groundstrokes especially, because they had always been the weakest part of her game. With all the practice, drilling, coaching, shortened strokes, and her increased strength, Billie Jean went home a much better tennis player.

Australia had not been easy, but all the effort had paid off for her. "At the end of each day I was really tired. Not just my body, but my mind, too. The whole thing was very discouraging. I would doublefault fifteen times a match with that new service and lose to just about everybody all the time. People told me, 'Go back to your old game. You can win with it.' But Merv made me believe that my game would get better." He was right.

She was now ready to take her place in tennis history. In 1965, she did not lose a single match to an American tennis player. She won the Pennsylvania lawn tennis championship, and the Essex County Club title. But as an international tennis player, she still had some problems. In the finals of the American lawn tennis championships at Forest Hills, she was once again beaten by Margaret Smith.

Even though she lost, Billie learned something very important. She knew that she could beat anybody. She also decided after losing to Miss Smith that she could beat her the next time. She felt that the following year would be her year and that she would walk away with the title.

After the Forest Hills tournament was over, Billie Jean Moffitt married Larry King. Her first year as Mrs. King proved to Billie that she was right in her feelings about her tennis. 1966 was a winning year! She won a series of tennis victories that included singles, doubles, and mixed doubles. She finally defeated Margaret Smith in a match in South Africa and took the tennis championship of South Africa. But her greatest victory of all was at Wimbledon, where she beat Mrs. Ann Jones of Great Britain in three sets. This win meant that the United States could keep the prize—the Wimbledon cup. The American team won 4 to 3 over their British rivals.

Back at Wimbledon a few weeks later, Billie took the All-England singles title for the first time. She now had come into her own as a tennis player. Billie Jean had become a professional. She was also a different kind of player. As she herself put it, "I decided to cut out any talking and think more. Talking does not win championships and I talked too much out on the court before." She said that she took tennis more seriously and that she had finally tightened up her game. She was playing the tightest tennis of her life and she simply swept her opponents aside. Her slashing stroke, her strength, her aim, and her energy were great. She knew that she was now the queen of the tennis courts.

When Billie Jean had left for Australia, she had said that she was leaving because she wanted to become the number one player in the world. She knew that

she couldn't do that and keep on going to school, too. This was not an easy thing for Billie Jean to do. Later on she said, "I was scared. Terrified. It's bad enough when you say to yourself you are going to be number 1, but when you tell other people—wow! You suddenly feel maybe you haven't got it. When you ask anybody if they want to be number one—win Wimbledon or something like that—they naturally say 'yes.' But they don't really know what it's like, and when they don't make it, it's awful."

She believed in herself. Her teachers believed in her. Her friends believed in her. Her husband believed in her. Her parents believed in her. And this had helped her to do one of the hardest things in her life: to become the very best in her field. She would not settle for anything less.

At Wimbledon in 1967 she kept her women's single's championship title. She also teamed with Mary Casals of San Francisco to win the women's doubles. And with Owen Davidson of Australia she won the mixed doubles. Billie Jean was the first woman to win three Wimbledon championships since 1951. Later, in September of 1967, she won the United States Grass Court title at Forest Hills in New York. She kept her crown as the world's top ranked amateur woman tennis player.

Off the tennis court, Billie has had a very good life with Larry. Billie feels that "it's probably better that we are apart so often. When we are together, we just enjoy each other so much, not much law gets read and I don't get much practice in. Larry does have his moments, too, when he gets asked for his autograph which he always dutifully signs 'Mr. Billie Jean King.'" "I don't get put on too much any more," Larry says. "The guys at law school couldn't believe it but they at least stopped thinking I was crazy." Billie Jean says to that: "I've told him if he ever wants me to quit, just say so. It's hard to stop, and it will be for me. But if he said that, I would have quit."

"When we were married, Larry said that it's a shame people don't use their talent. I agree. I think it's the worst thing in the world."

Billie Jean and Larry have both used their talents. She makes very good money playing tennis. She sometimes makes more than one hundred thousand dollars a year. Billie Jean is glad she is successful. She is very honest about making money. "Money is everything in sports," she says. "It has made me a star. I am hitting the same shots I hit years ago. But people are finally noticing me for it."

Billie Jean is noticed in many ways. She has been on talk shows. On streets and on airplanes people know Billie Jean by sight. The girl who couldn't afford to have a racket with gut strings now has her name on 17 different kinds of Wilson rackets. She has modeled dresses for Head, a company that makes clothing for sports, as well as equipment. She has worn socks for Bonnie Doon, another big company. Soon her name will be used for selling a brand of eyeglasses. Billie Jean's husband Larry takes care of all these money matters. He makes sure that Billie Jean isn't being cheated and that her money is being used wisely.

The money keeps them both working hard. And they are honest about that. They are also honest when they say that they are happy to be able to help the sport of tennis. But there is also something else they spend a lot of time on. They do not talk as freely about this, but they are very much into it.

Larry and Billie Jean are also trying to bring ghetto kids into the game of tennis. They are trying to open more free clinics and get more college scholarships for youngsters who do not have the money for these things. In this sense, the money is also a means to an end. Billie says this about the money: "Big money is the common thing. The guy in the factory can understand. He can put himself in my place. He says, 'If she makes all that much, she must be good.'"

Billie also remembers the reason she couldn't play baseball. She wasn't a man. Right now her brother is a professional baseball player but that chance was never given to Billie because she is a girl. One of the things Billie has done is to help set up the Women's Pro Tour. This was set up after Billie Jean and seven other women wouldn't play at a United States Lawn Tennis Association tournament. The reason they wouldn't play was because the purses, prize money, in women's tennis were too small. Billie feels that women's purses in tennis ought to have as much money as the men's purses. She thinks it is wrong for women to earn less money than men for winning at tennis. And more than that, she feels that some of the snobbery that people think of when they think of tennis should be done away with. She thinks tennis is a good, exciting sport that all people could play. Not just people with money.

"Women's Lob" is one of the key ways in which Billie plans to change the sport of tennis. Women's Lob is Billie's way of talking about Women's Lib on the tennis courts. Last year the prize money totalled $30,000. The winner of the purse was Ann Haydon Jones who won $9,000. That is about three times what a winning female tennis player would normally get. Billie Jean is very excited about "Women's Lob": "I'm a little rebel, I'm a little creep. For six years I've wanted us to go on our own. I thought we could make it—and now I think we have."

Naturally, there are a lot of men tennis players who think Billie Jean is wrong. Arthur Ashe and Stan Smith, for example, are two male tennis players who feel that women tennis players "should all be home having babies." But with the help of Gladys Heldman, the editor and publisher of World Tennis Magazine, the ladies have finally set up tournaments of their own. The ladies are very proud of their tournament because they feel that their game does not depend on who is the strongest or biggest to win. Instead, women's tennis has a lot more surprises. What women tennis players may lack in strength, they make up for in their ability to place the ball on the court.

Billie Jean is always right on top of this scene through her strong leadership. She speaks to youngsters to encourage them to get into tennis. She tells them that "I hope you make your career in this sport because there's lots of money in it." She usually breaks out into a wide grin when she says that. She tells other women tennis players that "we have to use our heads much more than men" because the men run the sport.

Through Women's Lob, Billie Jean and the other women tennis players have been able to give the sport much more color and humor. Usually there is no display of emotion on the tennis court. But the ladies on the tour have all kinds of tricks and habits; such as kicking tennis balls over fences, slamming rackets to the ground, and making comments back at the audience. Many people feel that this is a welcome relief. The great male tennis player, Poncho Gonzalez, supports the women's movement. Gonzalez says "Women should do more of the gestures they can make naturally—and get away with."

These emotional expressions can become very intense. One very well known French tennis star, Francoise Durr, bangs herself on her head after losing a point, shouting, "Oh, you stupeed!" And Australia's Judy Tegart Dalton gets herself ready for the game by whacking her own backside and shouting loudly,

"Come on, old fruit." The women also yell "Sorry" and "Too bad" to their opponents. They feel that women tennis players look more human.

Billie Jean used to get worked up too. Once a line judge decided against Billie Jean. She yelled, "How can you see from there?" The judge looked at her as if to say he'd been judging for 30 years and he called it as he pleased. But a little later, when he thought no one was looking, he moved his chair so he could see straight down the line.

Billie has settled down a lot. She feels now that it's most important to change how people think of tennis as a small private club. These groups are snobby and give tennis an air of snobbishness. This in turn puts off many people who would like to take up tennis. In the meantime, Billie keeps up her endless round of talk shows, articles, talks, and all the rest of it. In addition, she reads, dances, plays the guitar, plays bridge in her "spare" time. The queen of American tennis also says that she may return to college some day. She says she would like to get a degree with a major in history or in psychology. She points out that the only reason that she left college was that she could not both study and play tennis at the same time. Both things suffered. She also says that the chance for her to make money is right now. It is probably the best time for her to play. In a sport where to be thirty is to be old—and usually out of the running—Billie is probably right.

There are a lot of new young faces on the courts. Chris Evert of the United States and Evonne Goolagong of Australia have created a lot of excitement and have many fans. At one Wimbledon tournament some people were hoping Chris Evert would win. They thought a new heroine would be good for the game. "A better question is, would it be good for her?" asked Billie Jean. "I'm just starting to get the appreciation I should have gotten four years ago. I've waited a whole 360 days to make up for my last Wimbledon. I'm not about to lie down and lose for a storybook."

Billie and her husband still live very simply. They have a small apartment in Berkeley, California. They keep working at changing the sport of tennis. Whether they will really do it or not is an interesting question. Can two people change an entire sport? The answer is that it is still too early to tell. But it is not too early to say that Larry and Billie Jean have already made a good start in changing some of the problems. Billie now has her eye on much more than just winning more Wimbledon championships.

If she is successful, there will be more women tennis players who are treated as equals with men. There will also be more people playing on the tennis courts. She wants change.

Success has not spoiled Billie Jean. But not everyone agrees with her and her ideas for tennis. She says, "I don't think I've changed much. But I do things now and people nudge each other and say, 'Isn't that cute?' Well, I've always been like that; people just don't understand."

Billie Jean has held American, French, English, and South African world championships. Her place in the history of tennis is secure. She has also made it possible for more people to enjoy a great sport and for many young women to play in a professional sport and still play a lady-like game.

JACK NICKLAUS
BILL RUSSELL
MARK SPITZ
VINCE LOMBARDI
BILLIE JEAN KING
ROBERTO CLEMENTE
JOE NAMATH
BOBBY HULL
HANK AARON
JERRY WEST
TOM SEAVER
JACKIE ROBINSON
MUHAMMAD ALI
O. J. SIMPSON
JOHNNY BENCH
WILT CHAMBERLAIN
ARNOLD PALMER
A. J. FOYT
JOHNNY UNITAS
GORDIE HOWE

superstars!
superstars!
superstars!

CREATIVE EDUCATION SPORTS SUPERSTARS

WALT FRAZIER
PHIL AND TONY ESPOSITO
BOB GRIESE
FRANK ROBINSON
PANCHO GONZALES
LEE TREVINO
KAREEM ABDUL JABBAR
JEAN CLAUDE KILLY
EVONNE GOOLAGONG
ARTHUR ASHE
SECRETARIAT
ROGER STAUBACK
FRAN TARKENTON
BOBBY ORR
LARRY CSONKA
BILL WALTON
ALAN PAGE
PEGGY FLEMING
OLGA KORBUT
DON SCHULA
MICKEY MANTLE